this red metropolis what remains

also by Leia Penina Wilson

i built a boat with all the towels in your closet (and will let you drown)
Red Hen, 2014

Splinters are Children of Wood
Notre Dame, 2019

this red metropolis what remains

leia penina wilson

OMNIDAWN PUBLISHING
OAKLAND, CALIFORNIA
2020

Cover image: *Anguish* (1878) by August Friedrich Schenck

Cover and interior set in Wittenberger Fraktur MT Std and Electra LT Std

Cover and interior design by Gillian Olivia Blythe Hamel

Library of Congress Cataloging-in-Publication Data

Names: Wilson, Leia Penina, author.
Title: This red metropolis what remains / Leia Penina Wilson.
Description: Oakland, California : Omnidawn Publishing, 2020. | Summary:
"Answering a call to go feral, these poems are part invocation, part
prayer, elevating the confessional by exploring the nature of confession
from a feminist and anti-colonial perspective. A pop surreal romp
reckoning with lyric buoyancy through a mythic apocalypse, mysteriously
stark and playful. We meet voices trying to survive, reconcile their own
belonging, maybe, that drop in and out of a mystic narrative. What
happens in the aftermath of brutality? What do you do? The poems begin
to break down even their own authority. The landscape is itself too
unsettled; the form varies and reflects this endless transformation of
embodiment and interrogation. What can be recovered, if anything,
through an uninterrupted interrogation of memory, category, and
language-an unbroken attention to the speaker's own authority. Creating
an architecture and landscape that expresses both a ruination of
cultural time and an eternity of interior time, confession and lyric
become as much about the I as the you/we"-- Provided by publisher.

Identifiers: LCCN 2020023082 | ISBN 9781632430854
(trade paperback ; acid-free paper)
Subjects: LCGFT: Poetry.
Classification: LCC PS3623.I585483 T48 2020 | DDC 811/.6--dc23
LC record available at https://lccn.loc.gov/2020023082

Published by Omnidawn Publishing, Oakland, California
www.omnidawn.com   (510) 237-5472
10 9 8 7 6 5 4 3 2 1
ISBN: 978-1-63243-085-4

contents

apocalypse & carnival

in no certain terms we assassinate/ then we love

my own body   an enchantment

no one really believes

in/ the middle of the room

there's an apocalypse/ it's carnival themed/ one woman

decked out in turquoise glitter bells hula hoops hula hoops

another body dances knives/ who knows how it will end

it's hot here/ no cloud coverage no moist

heat coming beneath/ any moment might gulp us

mean desert flowers   thistle   & cunt/ has my life been intellectually
    thrilling

i wonder if it matters   the thirst   bodies all   slick of blood

dance whatever   of course/ there's a fire breather

a lion taming/ there's no more wilding/ mirrors

mirrors or it's so bright everything seems reflected/ or we're under water

with four suns more suns than i remember going to sleep with/ everyone
is having fun/ everyone is winning winning

nothing/ it seems/ surviving   yet

roar roar roar

this prize is yours   everyone is

going to die/ can you feel it/ the recognition
of what she is in other people's eyes

wearing that myrmidonian kings' leanlean skin/ i know

how it will end/ i infiltrate

cover my whole body & all my hair/ in food grade diatomaceous earth
this way i would catch them creeping out at night/ this way
something like a pact/ between sacrificed & sacrificing

apophatic rapture   wet/ leaves collecting/ there's grief
& some sort of/ denial

i've kept these vials of poison/ just in case
if you touch me

all the water will be sucked from/ your body
if you touch me

what a movie/ what a show

sister i adore/ a dystopian ending

are you excited by that instinct

have you fed on enough bitter plants

did you see the marbled polecat lost its prey

has the winter curbed your appetite for other animals   softbodied   how
    do we

reconcile the future   i'm taken aback by expression   by how expressive

i watch one grey centaur challenge another grey centaur

for dominance

over the rest of the herd

i decide i'll love the winner

they rear up

they neigh neeiighhhhh   it's just a sound

i don't know how to write it

they're so unified in their glee it's so malicious i'm certainly in love

i call the winner . best beloved centaur

best beloved centaur pledges allegiance   i love you i say

best beloved centaur neeiighhhhhs   shakes

that glorious mane all black almost purple so royalroyal

the loser's blood is all over best beloved centaur & i feel so hot

i love the love of dominance for dominion over body   best beloved
    centaur are we bad

survivalists   did i wait too long

when i smell those dead bodies   fuck me or get off

i want sleep i've had a long day & literally i can't stand

either of us right now my own pleasure   bored

i hate my wound

i eat it

my sister   total image of defeat

my sister   perfect bastard outside the rules

& i play a game   keep-away/ we keep wargods' soul/ send his body
    away

the crowds love this game they think it's temporary

for you i break each of his legs   watch/ i breakbreakbreak

do you remember   we used to tie strings around firefly legs

we'd forget to let them go   do you think everyone else forgot

how to express truth   there's not enough water/ and there's too much/

we're surrounded we'll drown we might not ever find land/ i pray for

winter/ i don't want/ this spoilt

this apocalypse/ an opportunity to equalize   lyrically blue the blue

segmented belly of a fat caterpillar that'll break its own body to be a blue

fat moth/ i think i'm going to kill them all/ i'm not even sorry about it/

cunts you've basked too long

let us enjoy what she says   *no one in love really believes love will end*   i
    think how true how tragic

we never called the other by name/ sister always sister my sister/ did we
   lose ourselves then

sister always my sister/ i dream nothing is unified/ what's all this soft
   matter for

i am delighted i am in pain—

that single poetic theme arewedestroyed—

can i turn my anger   back on something

that is not myself—

you were right   lust is sacred

romance is ritual—each word a crude woodcutting

of some romantic feeling or miracle lost or

any of those overly dramatic teenage urges

my centaur army—do not despair i do not die

i draw the arrow/ out into myself   the human way—

make them your meat—make them your meat

best beloved centaur says   eat your meat—eat your meat

i can see the fish in best beloved centaur's stomach

as another one gets knotted   tiny harpoon structures

triggered by touch   yet—

do i trust best beloved centaur—

i say another prayer   i want
to think   and speak   and move my mouth—

i fall back into world
there are too many words i don't know

what is said what are you saying—

yes—yes—love is meaningless—

i dreamt one of three moons fell
there were dragons—second apollo was angry & i breathed
fire   i wake/ appalled

best beloved centaur snickers
this is the kind of thing they like

with whose blood did i fill my grail—
with what red dreams
what did i defend myself against—
what lie is men's heart—

all lies best beloved centaur says *all lies*

we are culpable   the carelessness

of it all   wargod says don't

question a window about your sight—

i laugh meanly   don't yourself—

what a fucken mausoleum

wargod says—a lot of shit   i slash

wargods' tires   i imagine i let wargod die—

imagine wargod in a pile of wargods' own blood if wargod has blood

i imagine inside wargod is nothing—like just—beyond empty—

i feel frantic about it—i think if someone tries to save wargod i'll kill
them

i think just let wargod die just die—

the forests of home   will never be freshgreen

leaves are edible   and so are leafeaters

stroking the larvae waiting for them to secrete that blue goo   honeydew

beauty located around the eyes   one interior to another

tens of thousands of mouths   working in unity

to feed an underground garden

to feed themselves   vertebrate animals highly adapted

for flight   tsk tsk tsk   are you so

newly wild   basilgreen out of focus—

it's all pained   the colors pain   what is

the marker of this city anyway   what risk

is truth/ a wound   body

water   reds

& are we

cunt welcome to the halfworld/ everyone halfdead/ a quality i call loss
    birds

cut the sky/ into existence/ why   is a bird

all those myths/ cooped up—the limit of imaginations/ men are/ chicken
    is

tasty though all that white meat/ boneless/ what goes down in the
    kitchen/ i

suppose none of us look like animals anymore

this game is called *sound of distress*—she/ shucks his cock   now she has
    a cock

she says shuck a cock/ we can both play—o america   why/ is this

that awkward pit/ sweat my ambition/ its dry mouth/ how many bodies

has he worn through that wargod of yours/ a mouth full—

spit it out spit it out

the sun desperate—i desperate—it's all so desperate—

nothing recognizes itself/ the ego out/ a dead female

poet propped up against best beloved centaur/ what

to do what to do/ her body her thrice

tuned lyre her stained green sash—

the sun setting the sky purples blues reds/ aren't we sisters

look at her slouching there/ why do you follow

how many times must the world unfall—

in the name of love why even—let's not

digest it/ the desire to salivate/ what virtue

i make myself

drop the metaphor immediately

we build our own museums

we are each unsatisfied

i call mine grief   she *glory*

i think how like a boy   the object

of devotion   her abuse

his own likeness

we collect body

bodybodybodybodybody

i want to believe what she says

about fate

i know she prays to see your face one last time

if only we could freeze object of love in time

i wish i say   i wish

it comes down to a question

of ownership—the echo

of war

the education of achilles

the education of ponthesilea

who joins the war to grieve   are we not even allowed this

without violence

the education of hylonome

who we know—wanting

wanting herself dies

no longer desiring

this is education   is it always (like this)

i send a message/ every day icarus

icarus *icarusicarusicarus*

the world goes on   .

the people walk by still

the windows are opened still

still visible some black-throated loon —

the sun sets again

it will set again tomorrow

icarus your legs awkwardly twisted

icarus is that what they mean by head-over-heels

the tide wans

again the angler dresses their lure

again men disregard other men's warnings

the ships set sail

the herding dog doesn't even notice

the sheep are sleepy—

there's no way through this dream

i'm so sad with it/ the realness

what's the word/ reality

there's no real light anymore or is it

there's no real/ anymore—

i just had a vision

of how we know shit &

i am sick with my own thinking

discipline &

anarchy

i laugh   i am mean/ *icarusicarusicarus*

did i make her/ mean too

my mind is in danger i say

my body is an object i say

what price can you not afford to give

you don't understand anything i say

i recovered in the brine   nothing

i had lost

desire to desire

the future (of death)

how to get to

how thirsty

best beloved centaur aren't you thirsty

for marrow

a jagged ambush like red

we read

the crows the sheets

wore our whore (horror)

always stained always so fucked—hot

gurl summer   *exposition*: why not

your blood

wargod must have felt safe looking away like that

so surprised wargod forgot how

the drapes red

of course aren't we all

punished for our ambition   aren't we all

let's title this *bitch knows what bitch is doing*

now you can imagine me desire me

wine dark velvet puffed sleeves every young dream black lace — so
  fantasyfantasy

welcomewelcomewelcome — to the whole human life

my own grief i am

a body

always in three's   intentional   always the rule the exception

this whole human life — this *it's all broken so*

so —

a herd of walruses emerge from water

i watch them   hungry

there's nothing to eat there's nothing to love

i don't know the difference if i ever did

are you a demon sent to test me

how far—son of some glamour'd god—*how far*

stripped of those gold bands

without an offering of beauty   only your whiteness now—

now it isn't enough is it—

now none of the dreams are contained you can't contain them—

what are i   god it really is untranslatable

roughen up the darkness i say   cunt it up

celestial blue wisteria blossoms

all dehydrated

i say it again   a spell—celestial   blue wisteria blossoms

press one into another   into another

declaration of

stay alive stay alive

what work is trust/ sister is not used to failure/ who is really

i wonder if even now these/ words/ untrustable

sees something important/ stays silent about it

a centaur falls to the ground tramples their own murderer

i have dropped the honey pot am out of honey

i feel so many feels so useless about it

here's something important: he calls this one eurydice

she sits alone on a redred bed i sit next to her envy her redred hair

i say i saw a girl once with hair as redred as yours

she questions the efficacy of her own soul/ i slip my hand up her skirt/
    catch

her breath/ teeth seethes/ what void

we survived the dinosaurs i say how incredibly quaint

yes! yes! (i say) let's celebrate/ we lock lips/ assert each other/ who/ does

not love god/ who does not love love/ who would not raise this mace in

defense/ i promise you great friendship/ i promise you poetry so wild wild

teach me   against wickedness/ this high place/ this scorpions' tail—

unable to say that anything is definite/ i am ecstatic unknowing

sister in the midst of desire

your army is calm

send them to locate

our new needing

ambivalent sister   suppose destruction/ is already

on its way   are you/ really/ just

going to sit/ there

remainderless

the boning is difficult

taking the meat off   a crystal castle

every room of all seven chambers   a secret

place   what world within world within

overflowing with what

for what   i don't know anymore

anything   i don't know anything anymore

tomorrow we're debuting all the monsters it's easier if there's conflict

today we clean tiger cages because there's nothing else to do we wait for
    it

no one is coming to the carnival anymore

best beloved centaur is bored   i'm bored too   probably i won't

make it out alive i say

best beloved centaur snorts   i'm being dramatic yes

there's nothing else to be   i learn

tigers remember   an old newspaper tells the story of a tiger

who tormented by a zookeeper escaped one night opened his throat

went back into the cage like it was nothing

like it was nothing   i breathe that in   like it's palatable i imagine it
    tastes sour

some kind of texture i imagine tamarind

being able to vengeance whenever   *like it was nothing*

fuck it makes me so hot   another snort

37

i like tigers   i seek too—

a prophecy: those delicious curls do bite

our apocalypse   unhousing   something concrete

i want us to be feral i say

you don't understand love i say   i want us

each to be wild   in the wilderness

best beloved centaur snorts somewhat attractively

how is that even possible i think what is real anymore

sister   i carry you

uncombed

through smoke

& trees   & myth

using wings   known as bonds

how well the whole house   griefless

door   table

our azure & green couch

all those old things

what bitter   my heart

achilles is not a god   i see

the hideous noise of his cry

the softness of your learning sister kills me

i am unclothed   i challenge

the circle of red salt

with my teeth   i spill our blood

guard me against that spring

its twittering chattering

scrapping gutting   hush

of a blue-throated bird

the one-eyed goat knows   i try

to hide my loneliness   a river worn rips open

i am scared   we should all be as scared

my reflection   gives birth

lynx   leopard   tiger

pig   mole

& is forgotten

it makes no difference   when i

remove one or two impurities

the red stained

cherry blossoms

fall shortly

world   are we now

each in love

with ourselves

there is so much time

how would we know

she has one of those literary names

sister i don't like this

what would she succeed to

why're we always repeating ourselves

i am sick with it

that's an apocalypse for you i say

is this funny or fortuitous best beloved centaur says

is anything significant i say

magnificent!   magnificent witch   magnificent dying magical flesh boat

which mask   ourselves

can we love/ like this

will we return home

i am very tired

i am very tired

hating laughing reconciling

lover mother sister kin   the birth

of our child

is burning

conquest   & victory

conquest   & victory

i could have left this page blank history likes that

conquest   what bodies are visible

& victory   who is countered

what desire wanes/ what silence stability

some lesson in linguistics

i could supply a definition   history = striving to learn

what is taught in pain

here's how i read it—oh resistant grief! red mist!

o brutalized aesthetic! o morning blood!

o blood o blood o deep red menstrual blood!

o deep red menstrual blood!

o deep red menstrual blood!

o deep red menstrual blood!

o deep read menstrual blood!

what's the opposite of sex—

i don't know best beloved centaur says   unsexing

is that what you want—

hmmm i say

what fills my head—

they called these *ideas*

what are they now—

something like hope—

something false

something—something—like   we don't have

that luxury

do we—

let's unsex each other i say come here

yes

yes

yes

yes

what did they call this—consent

it gives me pleasure to observe your fears

observe mine too i say

observe too my pleasure

call to your deities   sea horse

i say *sea horse* like a term of endearment

like it's the sexiest sound ever to come out of any mouth

like if it's the last sound i make i might be happy

like i believe in happiness

like i am worshiping best beloved centaur *sea horse*

sea horse sea horse   i'm dying for you

call to your deities   hold them steady

hold them steady   a prophecy: the future

is right here   i'll behead them i tease

i'll turn them into stone

we'll fuck right next to their horror

right next to that moment when they know they're gonna die

and they die   and they can't do anything about it

this is how i flirt

hoof—hoof—hoof

don't be like that i say   let's be handsome

come closer

folding the wildness in   pressing each layer carefully

so the fat doesn't leak out

so the fat doesn't get warm   my sister *sister*   your wargod

is untrue   a/part from the fold of the real

take no lover—

i take no instruction (from the word) just the bone

how old was this mammoth when it died—*no no no*

how long did the mammoth survive

these feelings   an endless screaming into

the worn-out future   the void is it/ *the* void *a* void *this* void this red

metropolis what remains sacred   true

i give the signal for the slaughter to begin

the word   a want   something other than wings   newly body

murmuring what is intimacy

devouring—devouring—

devouring—

moth—

memory—

myth—

i can smell it

what's buried

there   needing to tend

sisterdesiring   calls to the rain

sisterothering   holds the child

as if she knows   it will do

horrible things yet

we cleave

each skeleton on top

another skeleton

another skeleton

another skeleton

another skeleton

creating a super organism

a super skeleton

i try to explain the relevance to best beloved centaur

best beloved centaur says can't we just trample over

i try to explain   there are more

of us   but each skeleton defers to

that one mouth

is an invasive thing

is not without a trace

is so much louder than

i look at all 12 books of prophecy and still/ no name

for this loneliness   i will not be docked by it

best beloved centaur   hold me tightly   we will not

inspire each other   yet

your body is so fascinating/ fascinates me

best beloved centaur says   i might a soul—

would you i say   i wouldn't

like you like that—

what does hephastus offer anyway   what they all offer

there's no body to hear her scream

no body no body no body no body no body

to hear   so/ i guess

scream

screamscreamscreamscreamscreamscreamscreamscreamscreamscreamsc

reamscreamscreamscreamscreamscreamscreamscreamscreamscreamscre

amscreamscream   could it be less

i don't know   controlled—can i (you) even ask that

it stinks

doesn't it

stark force of wound

bile breath

each blighted tree

sullied soil

reflection of thinking

hope is hard

the birds know

both day light and darkness night are faintly blue

glowworms or the flirtiest aurora   do you hear

the wolves howling

javelin ready   the curly tails of hunting mutts

follow the birds

is it gross or sacred i ask

might be hyena's

can't tell   which of us is deranged

it's familiar

a prophecy: the ground drops off

even wolverines

save half their catch

for the descending

do we wear whatoath

do we keep eachothersafe

sister the space between us

(the space between us)

this whole extrememeasure—

of hatredandmurder—

beasts without a head—

animals unaccustomed to the desert—

leaving it to perish on a branch—

something feline—

clutching—

the beautiful boneyard—

poem—

too sternly reluctant—

in yellowyellow terror—

of my pegasus   o pegasus—

those immediate feelings—

i generously love you—

i step away—

(menace)

i do not own—

(extinction)

you are dying   the advancing—

an accusation   the retreating—

a prophecy   a claim—

i don't like this best beloved centaur says   yet watches us fight anyway

it's necessary i say   i hold my sword like they held swords in really great

samurai movies when tv mattered like i was going to cut you into pieces

in seconds

like i danger & us   like   you looked at me like i could control the way
    you looked at me

it's okay you've survived badly   all men

have survived

wrong

don't worry

i won't flinch or i'd look like i flinched

didn't flinch moved so fast your peasant eyes couldn't keep up and before
    you could feel

pain you are dead so so dead

we burn more villages

take away more life

we even burn the trees

we are covered in dirt

& ash

& we smell

like all those things

honestly   sister i would like

a bath—

i would like to smell—

like helen   bruised apples

late roses   isn't that how you

described beauty

once   that familiar fragrance

masking the battlefield

once permeating our tragic history

our shit choices the hurt we've done to the other

could we pretend the world

less hostile   could we be new—

could we just not do this this violence didn't we like each other once—

&—

& could we pretend—

we would love each other—

could we pretend to love—

again   pretend we could be

friends even—

wargod uses each head to slay another beast

sister that's what he thinks of us/ even you

even in your winter finery/ our family gauntlets

bedazzled/ because one night we forgot

we were enemies

we forgot one head two heads

so many heads we couldn't tell which

was dead which was our own so many beasts   o beast

o beast o beast   i steal back each head

try each one on try to find my original head

was that a lie too originality i steal back what was stolen anyways

tell me how you survived i say

tell me i can survive too i say

dead speaks to dead/ don't you see

wargod comes for the assassination

what hazard

you choose

when the thrill is gone—such slaying

o the thrill the thrill

i wear homer's blood   each hercules hung on achilles' shield   now
    mine

each hercules hung on my shield—   ripening—   ripening—

here are the terms of my friendship—only fear those who fear

death will separate us   set everything else aside   love still

how else will we find our way back how else a path to follow how else
    forge

i don't like you like this best beloved centaur says this will not solve
    anything

there's no other choice i say   we can't wait

why   why is this sorrow nameless

don't worry sister   i'll come for you

i'll smote   smotesmotesmote

i love you &

i put wargod in our best nightmare   he'll never find you now

i've tucked him into the coffin locked him in the godblesseddark

& left

sister laughs at me

i laugh at her

we are both weeping now it's unclear if there's joy

is this what we are now

she resists   the language her mouth owns she tosses the corpse

what a waste best beloved centaur says

my heart beats beats beats

an arrow hits a bird the bird says it wasn't shot

we all weep at its courtesy

doubt its word

blood burning moons

uncertain form certain formlessness

one room to another room it's endless

i'm sad with its endlessness

feeling that you can't mother what you bring

each abstract turns on you   i am

some kind of demon

i die

the early nightmare is one snake turning into two snakes turning.into
   three very fast snakes

turning into four snakes turning into five snakes turning into too many
snakes to count now they don't even have to be fast there's too many of
them to outrun

each failure a challenge

i will not know benevolence

what is the saying out of all this beastly something must come sister replies icarus   such bravery

icarus

isn't that what death   is about   what
willingness to lose
each hunting dog
hunting a different scent
so much wind
we embrace
she prophesizes
capturecapture   the nature
of our authority   together
we excite
the wound
refrain from
mere survival
come
come   let us divide
conquer   a hero's strategy
isn't this heroic

i dig my fingernails into the earth while speaking and weeping

it's a party we rub

ashes all over the other's body

only the good know

flung green wilderness

it is the sound of goats talking

foolish autumn cicadas frantically crusting our branches

near oleander & pulpyfat

watermelon seeds spit the answer

is quiet robber take what you will

with vengeance   our flesh remembers

this gorgeous!

it's a golden crown

& it's grand

when i lay my ear close to the abyss i can hear its

teething   *sister*

keep the door

longing to be held

says Eurydice

don't you know anything anymore
an epic is a poem with history in it
what if   what if it's all gone
the experience
of the event   of the poem
as it was experienced —
that's what they do
alter the sounds
ghost the moment   wash it (watch it)
until it is wretched (wrecked?)
& what is the politically proper way   to say
dickbag
white & hetero normative   & cis gendered i suppose &   too academic too
many syllables too   let's simply say *male/yuck*   was i not
was i not supposed to notice all that *male/yuck*   i went
in fear
of abstractions   of being abstracted (extracted?)
why is it always   knowledge
a smiting hand —
i lost it
what if   what if
poetry was never there

here— i bound the spine
with poison   hoping
to take you with me
what is here
let's see

says Orpheus

you cannot prevent
how a man measures himself

the way he eats   the way
we imagine   after it

each ecstatic convulsion
a prayer   that grieving thing ,
i have come for it

i have come for you

that grieving thing
i am

says Eurydice

the hanged man (luck side up—depending)
the chariot (luck side up)
temperance (luck side down)

climate happening in your faceeeee   i do
all these mean things because i can
control them

i don't like myself
so i hate
like an extrovert

joke's on you
i stopped shaving
for life

my life cycle   no more
a flowering spring
recorded

says Eurydice

i took many animals
good   & true   & live

into my mouth
& am still in debt

if this is love then so be it
i forget what i am who

i belong to who do i belong to tell me
become sick

from the sight the love of
my memory

i hate my memory   of you
everything is in love

in love
you were better

this world is in love
everything is ruined

says Eurydice

you denied me my loud sound
that red laugh as if i was so faint of heart
as if chiron was not also my teacher
as if troy really was lost for a kiss
or a run of notes on a lyre
as if

says Eurydice

i can have no empathy for a hero
no matter how pious how rage how hottt

says Orpheus

what about   hottt
gurl summer

the big bad
wolf

is news   in addition
to the government bio

selective   hey
hey

don't worry
don't worry

says Eurydice

i've lived & i want
out

some squirrel eats a nut
shits   is satisfied

i cut   bleed
for days

how responsive
loneliness

says Orpheus

what is real
& what enchanted   is
knowledge evil
it's owned   it's private
privatized   that makes it sound
safe huh   what is genius anyway
art   without doubt
what right had i
over your gaze
am i the hero
radiant radiant death!
longing overcomes me—
i could not dig deep
i had only honor
my fierceness
i could not run away
i have murdered
why   have i
murdered

says Eurydice

how meant for death do i do—
what is it   to be   a body

in a body that dies the poem   opposite of language
opposite of my misreadings   the poem

without the medium   my own
corpse

i will stay here
i will stay here in my own corpse

my feminine foresees   what suffering
what isn't suffering   the luxury of

can't afford to be depressed
can't afford to express

well what
would you have of me then

the mother split in two
i say a eulogy for my sister

who died by fire
bending her life

to his
meeker lower everyday

feelings weigh   so heavy on my stupid heart
your doubt hurts me

i cut it out
fall down before you

all my friendships   unfostered
leak out

says Orpheus

in the name of love i wear this mask this body
what's the danger in chafing up against somebody else's love
in making it your very own

says Eurydice

will there be no end
to this imprisoning
of you

says Orpheus

there may be no end
to this imprisoned
you

says Eurydice

i will not
be imposed upon
by fine words

says Eurydice

you did not kill me
you killed the world
you voted against the world
you do always

says Eurydice

must it be love
i have felt this before
put my veil back in place
conceal me   please
by fever i'm a scholar
i serve my own treason   i want
to be someone

i don't
want context

says Orpheus

i could not let you stay
against my training i question my own allegiance—

we buried the bodies naked
it was a well-researched form of torture

all the days i gave to the pursuit of
stronger—stronger—stronger

faster—faster—faster
to the pursuit of wealth   really

what else was my education for—

tangled seaweed it's a wonder i didn't drown
i cut off parts of myself to surface

the water
so red so gelatinous all those days gave to a mess of thought

than a lover's love
a lover's hate   those wounds we have yet to make

you are too kind
you are not kind enough

have i not loved is that not sufficient
i drove my mother away i turn my face away

i turn away   to learn   what death is about

to learn a little   of how you survived
this incredible need to believe

says Eurydice

this real light
now undone

this red metropolis   each dream untending us
untendering what remains

this is a spell   of blood & pyre   my feelings for you
an etymology of   what word

my first grief   of strategy   of vision
are we diametrically opposed

have you made me too clean   calypso
we invented love   broke the rest of it

i'm tired   your gun is numb   hey
hey don't you know it's painful   cattle

the day is not safe

that's right my academic argument is you are untrained

why have you taught me
in opposition   the default

says Eurydice

you assume   that i desire
you

says Eurydice

you assume that i desire
you sexually   it's all you've been taught
that i am beautiful
that you want me
that you don't
that when i say i don't
want you it's code for *try harder try harder*
you hear permission to question my consent
i'm supposed to pardon that huh
poor baby it's okay you woke now huh
i hate you
for that
that you imagine
the appearance   & disappearance
of my body
that conveniently it's hetero when you're hot
that it's not when u need to emote
which means emotionally tax   these words
aren't even unique they're just what's happening
what's a poem when i must say what is happening
what have you done to it
my god you are that monster

what have you done
what have you done
what have you done
why do you continue to do it
why

says Orpheus

putting a door on a body

failure of return

what gets away from me sometimes

all those feelings we had

each of us dying

waking up

distancing   under the same roof

is that how we become

enemies   love is that how we became enemies

says Eurydice

let me tell you what i can afford

this is how we are enemies

says Eurydice

i murder i murder i
murder murder murder   i
murder   i murdermurder
over
& over
& over again over again
i murdermurdermurder
murdermurdermurdermurdermurder   o
murmur   what true light
reflecting in the pond   over there
that clean unreddened reflecton
were we ever her   ongoing voices ongoing
voicing   each outside   blue
out of bitterness   blue   so blue so blue
saying i know   i know where you are
i know where you are

says Eurydice

the wilderbeasts are coming

the crocodiles gather in anticipation

what do i know/ of that patience

says Eurydice

i repeat   have we not loved

the other enough

what real things   these bonds of love

you say why doesn't it sound natural

it's a border you're not willing to let go

must you too forever look back

isn't that failure

aren't you a failure   my body is its own pain so

i narrate it   alternatively   like the rest of the world i could watch

lightning fire inside a hollow

& imagine my doubt is not in my enemy's hands

they call my death sacred

i lose my good name

isn't that lust   the stuffed mouth

of a chipmunk

says Eurydice

more!

says Eurydice

my sister you don't get it

my lover you don't get it either

i'm coming for your wargod

for you   for you i won't tell you

where i bury it/ your body/ my fabulous animal

says Eurydice

you ask   why don't we just kill you
i say i wish we would
rise up

i say yes   yes i do
incant your death

says Eurydice

i run hard   by this deep snow i know
it is springtime—

sewn into my thigh you must
now be my subject

would that i could sing
a hymn that is worthy—

your mortal body
couldn't bear such heavenly excitement
you burst into flames

my lion's chrysanthemum head
my lion's voice boomingbooming
my anxiety that fragile *i hallucinate you best*—
drink this drink this

i do not want
to die dumb

we grew our own grief

this body is not

those azaleas that moon flower

those fleas.

in times of terror & magic & catastrophe &
wound & descent & red & cunt & desire &
manifestoes & vision & witch & divine &
invocations & memes & fidget spinners &
handmaiden's tales i turn to the prophet alice
notley who is of course not the real alice notley
but one of the ones i dreamt though i hope she
will pray with me nonetheless i dreamt we
were friends i remember you saying *we have*
nothing to live for except the approval of our
flesh=eating god so i turned to flesh=eating god
& ate it now i need to know if this was okay if
this too could be merciful

can this too be merciful #ALICENOTLEY i read about a tree whose whole body
is poison is this the lesson have we become the fruit of this tree dispersed across the
ocean current poisoning is there a spell 2 extract the poison 2 dilute the blood 2 call
the moon n2 me *moon moon moon*

#ALICENOTLEY maybe it's all a contamination maybe i like this contagion maybe it's all i've ever wanted 2 have the best halloween costume 2 just walk around *surrendered* your eyes glued over my own eyes 2 be with you so i can't see my own fear so i can't see anyone looking at me can only feel the feel of tears are they mine surely yes yes are they tears though

#ALICENOTLEY is a witch some secret secreting inherited knowings it's not a secret what's a witch some woman—full #ALICENOTLEY full of information & warnings sequins collages puzzles feminisms no no but certainly feministthought i have this dream where i'm cut open & i'm speaking & i wonder/if i wonder if it always has 2 be this way power i have this dream where i cut myself open & i'm not listening i'm looking inside & there's nothingnothing inside in an earlier version i wrote *power womenspeakingliving* yet now even alive i don't feel *it* whatever *it* is 2 return 2 yourself after 2016 after it seems like dreams dried up pressed into my eyes so hard i lose sight or i see only a dream & the flowers themselves nothing grows even after you've pressed them in moistured them my body container in the present moment there's no other way 2 live really there's only power & the truth & the dead & the dead black bodies & the dead brown bodies & the live ones—everywhere the sentence isn't even out the mouth before another body another truth another dead live one #ALICENOTLEY no secrets here but won't you tell me fearlessness & *something vivid* something vivid that can't be taught #ALICENOTLEY this is when i knew i loved you you witch you my own contagion i keep i keep coming back & wanting

#ALICENOTLEY is a witch what the internet says a witch is hold up i'll google it

#ALICENOTLEY is a witch the internet says a witch is a recent movie several movies a witch is witchcraft which is practicing magic a witch practices magic so is "magical" or a "sorcerer" the internet puts quote marks around magical because i think the internet is skeptical about magic a *witch* is divinatory paranormal magical superstition necromancy possession shamanism healing spiritualism nature ah yes all the things that are not a fact & also mythic a fact a story a worship worshipper of the occult a talisman some body more than one body who have *esoteric secret knowledge* are *complex* @wiki a witch is a picture of a few middle-aged white naked women hanging out in the forest or woods eternal & timeless & night they have unruly hair they are big uncontained unruly everywhere with whatever the joy is almost as big as the trees one of them has a pet cat or wolf witches have cats or wolves #ALICENOTLEY do you have a cat or wolf

#ALICENOTLEY a witch the internet says has power is that why a witch exercises her activism through her body her body is her power is that why they make us n2 witches then also 2 settle that power within the body within a stick that is used as an extension of the body 2 make magic wretched there so it can be broken burned limited 2 make delirious & sexual & then 2 damage that sexuality 2 shame & make it acquiesce 2 a system which has built itself on the subjugation of women black women brown women queer women underrepresented communities 2 make sure power can be killed there i dream about it sometimes death making each witch each body a talisman so it can be shattered it's easier isn't it 2 break a thing 2 exercise hatred over a thing an object a representation of an idea than a body i guess really it's easy 2 hate a body isn't this how sex & race & ability get coded or maybe white people just don't care i think more & more about the carelessness of white people what does a body represent what does it have 2 be 2 be threatening *nothing* nothing at all isn't it funny it isn't at all how we are willing 2 subjugate through language difference yet we are not willing 2 call an autocrat's language of conquest & violence what it is god we're so fucked we're so fucked up

#ALICENOTLEY is a witch too nature 2 be skeptical too unafraid of anything even hell—your marie gets thrown in hell because mean girls you say *the problem with the girls: they're afraid of this. though they cast me n2 it. it's just hell* it sounds so reasonable it's just a place not a state of being i wish i were as reasonable #ALICENOTLEY yes it's just hell no big & another part of me thinks perhaps out of fear in all caps IT'S HELL and then you say *i give up on being afraid & on sequential time. everything's happening all around me, not in a line* @15cultureof1 & your poem reflects this *not in a line* allaround because of that initial descent & i think of all the times my mom has said in other words 2 give up on being afraid because you can't change what you can't change she means being poor & also brown & i wouldn't change these things i'm proud 2 be samoan & it's sort of crushing—empathy. 2 be. a part of. the scene of. abject. your own poverty. 2 participate in it. i fear—isn't experience strange that way well i guess if everything is happening at the same time then there really wouldn't be anything 2 fear the future is right there or here i don't really understand this it sounds good doesn't it i'll trust you #ALICENOTLEY i wish i wish i could give up on fear

#ALICENOTLEY i feel sometimes my whole life is learning & unlearning & relearning fear & i think about the ways *race & class intersect in structuring gender* @patriciahillcollins @blackfeministthought the ways they intersect in structuring any hierarchy any dominance & i remember one of my sisters or me maybe had 2 tell this well-meaning 1st grade teacher at a school registration that our mom was indeed our mom i guess this teacher could only see brown woman light skin kid & couldn't reconcile the two but imagine with me saying over & over again no that's my mom no that's my mom no that's my mom no that's my mom no that's my mom #ALICENOTLEY & yet she still takes your arm & tries 2 pull you away until your mom notices & wtf she says wtf are you doing with my kid

#ALICENOTLEY i'm thinking the same thing right now wtf is the government doing with those kids & while trying 2 be discipline about this half life i feel so present active participle about it so anarchykathy kathy kathy i don't know who 2 submit it—disciple anarchy &

#ALICENOTLEY i'm never going 2 write a memoir i get 2 distracted i was saying something about fear as a means of governing important 2 resist the normalization of this fear as well i feel partly comforted by friends who are also shocked & outraged by the catastrophe that is trump + pence but i have 2 remind myself *that* feeling & that *feeling* is temporary & just solace (solitary illusion maybe) there's nothing normal about being comforted that at least the people you've surrounded yourself with are not authoritarian nationalists i caught myself thinking *at least a lot of people feel outraged by the appointment of nazi's in american government* but that is not the case not enough people are outraged not enough people are calling these dangerous present moments out for what they are being constantly & continually terrorized and starved by laws white people get on it

#ALICENOTLEY i was saying something about witches what is helene says (i made a note) *a way of leaving no space for death of pushing back forgetfulness of letting one self be surprised by the abyss*—surprise bitches! #ALICENOTLEY i'm sorry that was my first thought after abyss

#ALICENOTLEY what does a witch sound like i watch you on the internet & take notes a word is a unit of measurement a syllable is—yes a poet *says* breathes the spell out loud do you hear that that's me breathing too close 2 your ear for effect (affect) for what fiction calls drama here's the drama activate the space make the circle *enough* that there's no threat of breaking it activate the space every time like a jellyfish carried in the sea that sucking expellingsuckingexpellingaction like i might ring my new alter bell the reverberation reverberates reverberates can you see the sound when it touches you it's in you now

#ALICENOTLEY you say the myth of rescuing the future @disobedience does not exist because we are present you are so right it is on fire *the house so full of garbage is on fire* @143 we must not let it become myth they'll be no stopping it #ALICENOTLEY &

#ALICENOTLEY is a witch a part of art or does a witch create art can you be both the object and subject of your own making where o where o where is agency in this mess it's again a question of distance huh can i make myself the subject of my art my poem & still be in control am i asking other people 2 read me then am i inviting other witches over can we cast spells together 2 figure this out does that even matter your poet speaker invents the arts invents *the art of seeing one carries about a transformational or formational tool the greens & blues the golds with which a lion or eagle was justly seen, existent in me. a space in which raw maroon or red is invented, either first* @5cultureof1 #ALICENOTLEY the work of the witch then here is the poem itself truth: i am—tired of this insistence on invention i see the forms everywhere i import them in & translate the poem n2 some form but that's too many words i guess i'm tired of the vocabulary of course i like 2 participate in the making of my ownness my own muchness that's the joy of any archival work undeading it i am tired honestly though idk of channeling the dead things

116

through my own body of pulling it out of translating the preverbalether & i wonder about authority again am i translating or is the vocabulary translating me & i'm so afraid—i—you say *i entered the bureau and cried. they were trying 2 rename me again. my greying hair was cut short…*& & *parenthetically you are an immigrant as well as a woman, don't expect too much* & here the poem becomes the body a body in the process of being revised my body my mother's body o mother don't cry don't cry i will cut my hair short too i even wonder #ALICENOTLEY at my choice there *revised* i should have thought first a body in the process of becoming so i wonder now how have i revised my body what i have done 2 be appropriate what have i done 2 this dying machine

#ALICENOTLEY a witch invokes a repetition stressed & unstressed syllables your particular sound syntactic texture in another essay i might consider gertrude & types of sounds but here autocorrect tried 2 assert *syllabus* ha silly bus a line break a broken visual syntax our hero activates *disobedience & no doctrines!* nothing is okay i am concerned with dismantling oppression

#ALICENOTLEY i know it's obvious terror & terrific are so close if i blink i misread one as the other

#ALICENOTLEY you incant *you can't reduce me 2 my organs* & in the same poem @theacquisitionofthesenses *i was located & so i might die* & in this poem like so many of your poems there's always a tyrant a supreme wielder of oppressive power even the mean girls & leroy telling lies trying 2 interrupt marie's transformation trying 2 exclude her from her own narrative from her own desire #ALICENOTLEY a witch is 2 be desired & they are excluded from desire don't desire yourself that's advice for survival & don't break a vow i think that's death that exclusion god desire & death desire & death desire & death i'm so tired of it all won't you locate me #ALICENOTLEY i spent all this time falling in love with hilda's helen & i wanted 2 stay there in the wanting warm excess its own discipline anarchy a witch a disciple of anarchyexcess

#ALICENOTLEY o desire so many of these images of witches are connected 2 desiring conjuring a thing some object 2 own calling n2 realness the physical & i'm thinking now about #disobedience when you say *but now, now it's so hard to work for history...* and i am struck by the wound of our historical mediation 2 be mediated witch no what's inside me even who put it there did i let it stay & also *one may be smarter than history, forever, as one's smarter than the media, or the university* @146 & i want this 2 be true for us 2 be smarter than those institutions but looking at the world now perhaps that was our tragic flaw me thinking (ha jk jk) me thinking that we were smarter all along when we weren't what is it anne says re: desire herself probably a witch *plato is concerned with 2 types of damage. one is the damage done by lovers in the name of desire. the other is the damage done by writing and reading in the name of communication* @erosthebittersweet @130 so much damage done on the territory called body body body body body

i wonder #ALICENOTLEY what plato knew of desire even what he knew of women's desire & i feel so vicious with god fuck u plato fuck u

#ALICENOTLEY when that living brushes up against somebody else's idea of how & what & who you are allowed 2 be *witch* i'm going 2 say it again *witch witch* say it with me *witchwitchwitch* an accusation or an invocation witch #ALICENOTLEY you say *do you believe in this stuff or is it a story* then *i believe every fucking word, but it is a story* @74cultureof1 & i think of all the tv witches i've seen charmed or the mists of avalon or the craft or the sailor scouts or any magical girl those women had such power textured power—she-ra! visible power such *resistance* what am i resisting do i always have 2 be resisting something do i have the luxury 2 i don't know just 2 exist here i hear helene say *woman can be far more effective and dangerous when socialized as wife, mother, or career woman. the unbridling is then changed into crafty reckoning, hysterical spells turn n2 murderous plots, extreme masochistic poverty becomes a commercial triumph* @168powersofhorror & i think fuck socialized fuck civilized where are the woods i will go 2 them burrow & also i fucklove all the princesses of power

#ALICENOTLEY i have a question what is truth the nature of how else 2 interpret the mediation of my own feelings—i—the scoring—this illustrated pain i try 2 seethrough the location is another question quest: of suffering it causes/a record—"*a woman*" "*& her child*" "*walk towards*" "*me*" "*they're on fire*" "*continuously on fire*" it doesn't end *the being—on fire* mostly the risk of it it's intolerable life is gertrude says *there is singularly nothing that makes a difference a difference in the beginning & in the middle & in ending except that each generation has something different at which they are all looking at* which witch am i looking at #ALICENOTLEY well i think we're in it again the epic again don't you feel it the call 2 epic again 2 participate in the public poem in the poem about having 2 explain settler colonialism again in class everything is fine fire fine fire what a fine fire all i want now honestly is 2 make book lists 2 be alone there are so many new epics & i love them all later if you want i'll make a list

#ALICENOTLEY another search reveals that a witch is another picture a picture of the wicked witch of the east who gets a house landed on her by a young girl from kansas a witch is wicked then must be punished by accident so it's okay so there's no true blame & a witch doesn't look like the young girl from kansas nor is she particularly beautiful a witch is either plain enough 2 be anybody or so different enough 2 stand out from the pervading ideal of beauty a witch is some ideal holding power—is *is*—she's inhuman she has a crooked long nose her nose is green her face is green we are not supposed 2 like green faces even though it's a common color in nature we are supposed 2 suspect nature the witch is supposed 2 die #ALICENOTLEY all those grimm-brother hansel & gretel witches who want 2 eat kill trick steal children die all those women in the forest or woods it's always in the woods go 2 the woods is that where the power is where 2 learn disobedience from everything 2 *take back some of what the novel has stolen from poetry & further,* 2 *avenge our sex* 2 avenge ghouls i mean women whenever i say ghouls i mean it's sort of crushing. empathy. to be. a part of. the scene of. the way i want. to be my own cunt. *for having—greatness—stolen* @174 #ALICENOTLEY i won't lie here i am all about vengeance & i wonder if i need some of this for my own survival whatever benevolence can spare what benevolence can a witch spare

#ALICENOTLEY i got a cunt crop top & in my imagination i wear it everywhere & no 1 notices because it's cool 2 be a cunt & every1 wants 2 be a cunt

#ALICENOTLEY one of my first academic lessons in disobedience was from audre lorde when she says *the erotic is a resource within each of us that lies in a deeply female & spiritual place, firmly rooted in the power of our unexpected or unrecognized feeling* & then *of course women so empowered are dangerous* @sisteroutsider & i felt dangerous for the first time & i wonder where that went #ALICENOTLEY a witch's power is within her a witch is dangerous *i'm coming for you* i whisper 2 my computer screen as if i'm dangerous right now isn't this my role 2 threaten you 2 have you come after me 2 take my head as those male heroes do 2 use my head 2 slay others is this the narrative headless heedless slaying if i were a gorgon before i died i might have said *there is no glory in this suffering; it is not an ode: it opens up only n2 idiocy* @kristeva & i would have died being correct yet dead yet dead

#ALICENOTLEY sometimes i want 2 shout & shake people & say *why* is your imagination so tiny & also *ahhhhhhhhhh* as if by shaking them i might be able 2 break their imaginations open just a little bit you know enough that it continues 2 be jarred open i'm thinking now of those last lines in the descent of alette—alette asks, & i feel myself as reader instantly reject, *"must we continue" "to live in" "this corpse of him?"* @148 are you shouting with me no no i want—i want 2 vomit i think nonono i don't want 2 live in the corpse of him i reject it even though i don't know who *him* is i reject the patriarchy of it all the misogyny & i wonder can't we be infected with a different masculinity—i really do hate men & i want *herland* charlotte was onto a thing but i suppose that's not sustainable so—that it's always violence violent that it can't just be tension it's always conflict must be conflict— conflict—conflict i feel sick with conflict can't we build our world somewhere else perhaps like marie maybe let it burn down the fire healing o the healing fire it doesn't heal anymore it's just fire a real scorch scorcher

#ALICENOTLEY i'm not interested in the sacrifice or abnegation of the female body in order 2 heal anything that moment when alette is reborn with her owl feathers the palebloballencompassing tyrant's blood no longer running through her veins i cry weep laugh joy in joy gross recognition of her victory even though it's alette's victory i look around for someone 2 share this moment with

#ALICENOTLEY witches are powerful that comes up in the google 2 & magic is a part of power but even a witch has 2 live in this world on this earth leroy has this fascinating moment when he says *i could never stop...partly because i wanted 2 stir them up. i wanted 2 see them have feelings—but i wanted the power. i never made them better, in my stories, than they were: only worse...* @96 here he starts 2 *feel guilty for every lie; he starts 2 remember them all* & i think i can't forgive leroy for these lies for the violence he's done maybe there's some way 2 make sure others don't become leroy *i could never stop* i keep thinking about that line power is perverse it's systematic it weaves itself in & we don't realize all the tiny privileges that make up our daily lives but sometimes a risk not the same as privilege but still there you have 2 risk it in the poem it's all i've got do i make currency of my own pain do i care idk i need to make visual & concrete my compulsion 2 participate in the reading my own serious descent what was it #ALICENOTLEY *walk straight into the dark & stay awhile* & leroy gets cured by a rattlesnake bite in this poem—leroy is lucky you're a benevolent witch—& says *my snakebite: venom cures venom? for there was that too, i hated them: why? because we were all too dumb* & i remember something you say later @cultureof1 *i think of the presumption that i am dangerous, a poet possessing dangerosite, who can intuit his emptyhandedness. a painful orgasm outside the bus of ruthless politics—* @139

where do i get enough snake venom #ALICENOTLEY i wonder if in the future it's funny 2 say it like it's a destination i wonder if in the future like in nevada or

in missouri or in alabama or in pittsburgh if that'll be something amazon stocks—
snake venom—wouldn't that be funny can't you see it at the whole foods

#ALICENOTLEY as a witch i'll pray 2 you do not let me be too dumb 2 understand
power is particular @audrelorde

#ALICENOTLEY the etymology of witch itself tricky as nobody seems 2 agree on what *exactly* the root is wei—weig—weik—wihen—vicis—wechsel—& so forth @ theinternet @wiki the old english is *haegtesse* meaning witchfury where the word *hag* most likely comes from why is it even a word what does it seek to contain *witch* witch & hag are often interchangeable hag itself means *of uncertain things* & also hedge i like this because it implies a trickster & a trickster in nature & in that the ability 2 shapeshift 2 transform body 2 adapt a witch adapts a witch transforms & is transformative her nature is uncertain her origin is uncertain she can make herself remake herself the powers are within her 2 shape reality 2 decide the terms of the real aren't restricted by anybody else's imagination fuck it makes me so hot so wet aren't you

#ALICENOTLEY 2 set one's heart on 2 do & do & do & do & do & do & do magic

#ALICENOTLEY is a witch magic or does she possess magic

#ALICENOTLEY i am sad what magic has survived the greeks what practice
what ritual phaedra's old nurse insane lovers fury-seized demons vengeful achilles
a story of men & sadness sure but by their own folly, must i sympathize—in an
earlier version i thought *empathize* but that has been used up, if ever—vengeful
crossed-lovers lost loves true loves untrue love real-life-some-shit-internet-stalk love
mediocre love isn't all love idk today i'm only n2 the queer love the sit-in-a-room-&-
want-love love we don't even have 2 want each other just want that's enough love i
don't want 2 share my body with anyone i please it enough love of love love scorned
love not returned amorous jealousy—medea i love you everyman's hero odysseus
even you hector even you hector stupid paris stupid helen 2 think those men would
let her own her own body stupider still—the afterwards holding helen's story captive
historically making policies based off myth the wrath of a goddess the envy of a
goddess the lust of a goddess a wanton an ideal we couldn't be anyways more than
your whore & even that you guard against that delirium rather than gods demigods
charlatans fortune-telling nomads @janeellenharrison is that it—*doubt* the untrust
of our own body our own desire the making of a monster the same as the making of
a woman of a girl we learn that *mageia is the service of the gods & the same man who
teaches 'mageia' also teaches kingly duties* @76 i laugh at that—that a man could
teach any of those things i mean *look at it historically* i imagine you're laughing
too i mean come on it's funny/absurd a witch is magic & magic had 2 do with the
divine & a knowledge of magic was required 2 rule but what survived the greeks was
disbelief—idk my family is superstitious which is ironic 2 me because superstition
implies that you believe in something but the rest of the world disbelieves ironic
also the latin factura means magical means *making* & i wonder why would anyone
disbelieve *making* it's such a tender gerund i just want 2 invite it n2 my embrace

hold it softly so i'd like 2 posit superstitious 2 mean cautious of the spirits & that's

right perhaps we should be more courteous of spirits

#ALICENOTLEY when you say *he invented you badly* @86 i know those stories about witches not from witches are slander are ways 4 men 4 tradition 2 control the narrative 2 stifle the power of witches are ways 2 warn us away from our own power i know we must—some imperative—*respect strangeness, otherness… 2 catch the most of what is going 2 remain preciously incomprehensible…that i like, that i can admit, that i can tolerate, because really there is always a mystery of the other* @cixous ok yes & the mystery of the other can be also exoticized so be careful out there that i must *devise a world in which my imagination actually participates* @84 but i never knew i was that otherness until you taught it me hmm learn & taught what culture has incubated grown flourished sometimes i feel very psyched about the harvest & other times i'm tired of it this consumption so here i am trying 2 get out & away yet still still putting things in my mouth

#ALICENOTLEY i want 2 believe we can build a world where each imagination can participate but i read somewhere that you can revise a poem but not the world the poem is written in/within so where does that leave me what do i do do i write more poems can i revise the world this way each poem its own invocation its own location of suffering can we write enough poems 2 address that other *emotion of exceptional trust which in timid people takes the place of love* fear @celine

#ALICENOTLEY a witch posits messy questions

#ALICENOTLEY is a witch is emily dickinson a witch she did say she doesn't have a mother don't witches never have a mother or do they always have multiple mother's i think it's both you're a witch if you have no mother or if you have lots of mothers or if you can't remember

#ALICENOTLEY is it always a question of origins

#ALICENOTLEY i'm very dull i worry about this i also know it's not the pain or suffering or whatever trauma that makes a thing interesting all this whatever can be so boring i mean just look at all the tv

#ALICENOTLEY i talked 2 my mom on the phone this morning about cheesecake she really likes cheesecake so i sent her one for mother's day so i've been thinking about mothers too in general also because my sister recently is a mother it's weird not weird-bad just weird thinking of my sister as a mother she'll always be *my sister* & now she'll also always be *zoe's mother* & i thought about those roles what they are each allowed about 'taking a lot in' about what exactly i've taken in without being conscious of it & i wonder if it even matters perhaps this is magic everything that we take in unconsciously @yousaythissomewhereinaninterviewontarot everything we feed n2 our own invocations those echoes of other spirits or ghosts or ghouls those faint trances of something else softly pressed

#ALICENOTLEY newly i've been reading the journals of sylvia plath & this is certainly another book but i wanted 2 drop a line—*i am so hungry for a big smashing creative burgeoning burdened love* & i've realized

#ALICENOTLEY speaks from dead 2 the dead her fellow ghouls

#ALICENOTLEY a troupe! a musical group a club that meets on a day & we all sit quietly in our own locations & we sing what would we sing—*it's not right but it's okay i'm gonna make it anyway: ah ah ah ah stayin' alive stayin' alive stayin' alive: you can dance you can jive having the time of your life* haha other songs from my childhood that time my youngest sister + brother were in gloria jean's coffee reliving our lives & the backstreet boys played (because the gloria jean's is a time capsule) & we just started singing *you are my fire the one desire believe when i say i want it that way* very very loudly haha!—i'd be dramatic about it i'd imitate the kings of old i'd ask 2 be sent four magic advisers i just read about this *magic advisers* or is it magical advisers i'd ask like those kings for the wisest one for the one most just for one who is most prudent i could use some lessons there & i'd ask for one who is the bravest because of all these roles i'd like 2 be brave

#ALICENOTLEY will it ever stop raining i go outside wait for the drowning this morning my tarot reads wheel of fortune (luck side up) the empress (luck side up) death (luck side up) #ALICENOTLEY what does this mean all this luck i just want to feel something & yet no i reject my own feels

#ALICENOTLEY a witch's imagination is not restricted by society or culture or any magnifying ambassador of idea or truth or whatever i hear you say *what is*

140

culture? it's an enormous detailed lie lived in, wrought beliefs, a loving fabrication.
what's good about it? nothing. it keeps you going, but it institutionalizes inequality,
killing, & forced worship of questionable deities; it always presumes an absolute: if
no other an absolute of intelligence & insight & also the lore of certain people—
men—what you're referred 2 @74cultureof1 sometimes i have nothing 2 contribute
because you've so perfectly captured the heartlessness of it all

#ALICENOTLEY the lure of men—ha! i say let the fish take them away i'll prep
another meal

#ALICENOTLEY where is it—my witch do i have 2 pull her through my own body too—the magic—poem: a purifying ritual *my city is the poem* dido says dream stifled by expectation—lady poverty says she's *getting poorer* yet also *sharper, more astute* & i understand this all those pizza coupons we kept these pancakes my mom used 2 make all that rice & ketchup packets & saimin

#ALICENOTLEY you say what is money marie says & what dignity is lost in the exchange this exchange i sigh & i'm the rightful owner of my own container annamarie you're right sometimes i do think myself outside these categories yet here i am building this container around myself i'm just going 2 let it all in so much it seepgroans out loudly like when you pack a bag too tightly & you try 2 take something out but it ruins the whole thing even if i you can't understand how here i'm letting it all ruin here & bask

#ALICENOTLEY the liminality its all a floating signifier thinking the body constructed judith says *demands a rethinking of the meaning of construction itself* & i say *please*

#ALICENOTLEY a witch learns stores what's the last one: transmits my upload is slow i hate all the institutionsofmen fuck gender but i understand there are consequences my reiteration lags i am uncertain how 2 witch the uncertainty of my own future the recovery of it what is it you say 2 medea dido cassandra 2 *break & recombine language is nothing 2 break & recombine reality, as in a dream, might be something* @somewhereinthesubwayonwaybackn2cave

#ALICENOTLEY it's not comforting so i think *must be true* a witch must be true

#ALICENOTLEY behind comfort there's something important i think as i read *there was power in that room. i saw/ it, because my eyes were crushed out/it's my judgement on this almost face/holding the mouth so & who matters it died & the magic & on its part i utter anything know it's in my unlawful hand for i choose a form not easily seen @3* & #ALICENOTLEY i see you #ALICENOTLEY i see neither you nor medea nor even dido by the end approve of that life of comfort i see you do not approve of silence that war that killing how comfort kills & #ALICENOTLEY as medea's body is investigated by the coroner as the autopsy happens & i think of all the ways newsmedia perform autopsies of black bodies & communities especially after police in america have murdered & continue 2 murder black people—from early august i add: *thinking too of hawaiians protecting mauna kea* & it's always a black a brown an indigenous body at stake

143

#ALICENOTLEY there's so much a witch could cast & idk you were right the world exists it is bad & super real

#ALICENOTLEY i know you're not dead & she's live as he autopsy's her body
& i am sick i think i'm watching the autopsy that body investigation & i am sick
again as dark ray says *i have 2 be a scientist in order 2 keep cutting her open; i can't
go off n2 myth. but i need 2 know where she's been—the murders are so necessary*
@44 & #ALICENOTLEY you are telling me that i the reader the coroner have no
control over you medea the ghouls even if you are dead *i am a ghoul, & i preserve
my remains by living* @45 i have 2 feels 1 i'm dead 2ice a woman of color samoan,
some 1st generation trying to figure it out, alongside intergenerational poverty 2 i
would like 2 keep-on preserving 2 ferment

#ALICENOTLEY untame my language o no it doesn't really belong 2 me does it
who owns the vocabulary how owned does that mean everything i say out loud is
owned what if i shout what if i shout will that unown my words unown my sound
i'll always shout if it makes you feel good you should shout too right now out loud
#ALICENOTLEY because i know you collage every time i read alette i see her you
cut cut cutting away that male mythos the tyrant's mythic body each *cut—cut—
cutting* a ritual magic that acknowledges a frame & cuts it away & allows access 2
something else & i hear gertrude *saying let me listen 2 me & not 2 them/can i be
very well & happy/can i be whichever they can thrive/or just can they not* @stanza3
& i think yes yes yes yes yes @kathyacker language doesn't break the code speaking
what the code prohibits breaks the code @empires & then even then—idk

#ALICENOTLEY welcome 2 my fancy welcome 2 the witch hot happening now

#ALICENOTLEY u ruin me

#ALICENOTLEY you break whatever is left

#ALICENOTLEY you are keeper of knowledge keeper of dead keeper of magic your power medea's power comes out of her body it stands as a ghoul against wealth against war against weapons against what thepoetthinks they know against what thepoetaccepts without question what others have told them is true even i guilt of this #ALICENOTLEY you said you don't believe in ghosts you believe in some afterlife what might be called the soul that a soul as medea as dido as alette as the first woman as marie a soul never dies & there is no god in god so none of the souls ever have 2 answer 2 an ultimate power a tyrant's power nobody's soul is subordinate nobody's soul is worth more nobody's soul can be used as currency

#ALICENOTLEY inanna! inanna! inanna!

\#ALICENOTLEY i scream & scream & scream & scream & i am still not loud enough

#ALICENOTLEY a witch—typo: sentence as entrance—in trance, medea dido alette even marie homeless—how with scarcity they're raging & trying 2 breathe surrounded by wealth how they're trying 2 breathe & the wealth—scarcity & what survival—another lie exhausting all the ghouls o glorious this glorious american capitalism #ALICENOTLEY does it always come down 2 a question of ownership how much one owns #ALICENOTLEY is this then a question of authority

#ALICENOTLEY i feel beside myself aside from myself if i feel anything i feel i want to be

#ALICENOTLEY power powerlessness marie can't remember why she wants 2 build a codex *a true dump manuscript, a book of pages of any paper* it's important this witch desire 2 *make a new world of one, out of our desperation, her talent* @30cultureof1 & immediately i hear *writing is inseparable from becoming* @ deleuze & i don't want to *make* out of my desperation & my talent—& immediately again reading here becomes a process of finding a descent each poem each rat stacked upon another poem so that i have 2 dive dive dive n2 it without knowing anything & the speaker doesn't know anything either *i don't know anything* & we don't know anything together also *i am mercy; i have no understanding of who i am; though, with my thousand arms, i have written of my own nature since writing began. i inhabit you & you write about me again* @3cultureof1 & i think yes marie mercy eve love lying leroy i am writing about you again mercy is mercy a part of *being* & is mercy a part of being a witch

#ALICENOTLEY we watched all the same tv all the same witches what happened

#ALICENOTLEY is mercy a certain kind of human magic

#ALICENOTLEY honestly then i don't think i can ever be a witch if mercy is

poetry's providence

#ALICENOTLEY i go looking for a witch in a museum an art i see many

#ALICENOTLEY i stare @ this red lobster wearing figure creaking a door a table a prism uncertainty here an argument maybe certainly i'm anxious but i can't look away are they live or dead motionless silhouetted captured by the shadows captured me am i live or dead will i float

#ALICENOTLEY witches dive n2 the wreck adrienne was a witch too the book the camera the knife blade diving & discarding becomes a form of revision & each time marie's home is burned down she rebuilds revises & i think how mean how necessary

#ALICENOTLEY if i were a witch i'd want more than this halfformed discipline & anarchy

#ALICENOTLEY i don't know anything about ovid or if he was a witch i think now of how his poem is also a constant site of revision a collection of the collective that *culture of one* which makes marie vulnerable & demonstrates her great great generosity she says 2 *remember a thing you have 2 analyze yourself* @99cultureof1 she doesn't *want 2 close this world in* this is one of many moments where we're asked 2 question the world outside the book 2 *remember how 2 suffer; remember the philosophy of screams* @115cultureof1 & i also recall the ghouls eating from blood sacs warning each other through history 2 *see past the smoke of disastrous fears* @ songsandstoriesoftheghouls #ALICENOTLEY a witch is continually asking us 2 consider the limitations of our words how they've been coded how we wield those codes in our lives on whom do we use them even i know *witch* is a word & it sounds ungenius 2 say words so coded can be weapons words so coded can be weapons words call n2 question themselves #ALICENOTLEY yesyes magic magic magic allows us 2 think outside this frame 2 reconsider all prior citizenships 2 come up with ways 2 break expand break break break #ALICENOTLEY a witch is deeply critical of words this does not come up in the google

how suspicious we should be #ALICENOTLEY of the ideas basted onto the words that call n2 question our own selves

#ALICENOTLEY a lot of the world perhaps all of it seems 2 be a question about trust & vulnerability & all the games between i'm not saying games as in let's have fun i mean games as in something is always lost what is won really would you agree trust & vulnerability as i read marie's story i keep coming back 2 those words *your house—against the house* @59 it feels sprawling & empty is that even possible #ALICENOTLEY you know the first time i thought i could be a poet i was eating spaghetti out of a container my sister made me for lunch on campus in rural missouri a woman with big great red hair witchy hair curly hair walked up 2 me & said my spaghetti looked good & i offered her the container & someone said she was mary ruefle & i thought good thing i offered her my container she's mary ruefle & i vowed i will always offer all my spaghetti 2 her even now she said *ramakrishna said: given a choice between going to heaven & hearing a lecture on heaven, people would choose a lecture* @fromapostitnote & she pauses here 2 let her audience consider heaven or a lecture on heaven & i find myself wondering what would i choose an experience or hearing about hers & i thought mary what a trick you've played you witch you beautiful beautiful witch & i choose heaven #ALICENOTLEY i choose heaven

#ALICENOTLEY i hate men sometimes i say that as a joke but really in my heart with everything i've ever believed in i mean it men disgust me i know it isn't fair 2 hold each male accountable for their whole horrible history of silencing women's voices or for silencing voices of women of color or my mom tells a story about missionaries coming to the island & i find it hard 2 hate missionaries except that's how they get you 2 believe the rest of their domesticated shit if i learned anything from my mom's stories it would be 2 resist domestication #ALICENOTLEY i was once at a picnic where one of those white men asked me where my family was from & i said samoa & they said somalia & then there was awkward silence because he thought he was being funny he thought i was going 2 laugh like he was laughing & really can you believe that *laugh* & i was trying not 2 throw my drink in his face then rip said face off with my teeth & i know i shouldn't think violence first but i was startled n2 it so startled all i could think was violence how irrational & at moments like this i also think the world hasn't changed so much #ALICENOTLEY you said we have space now but no prestige no power tell me how how how

#ALICENOTLEY witch prophecy is prophecy a part of witchcraft do witches have prophecies my mom has never spoken 2 me about witches but she talks about spirits & dreams which is like prophecy prophecy & dreams & spirits & ghouls all this supernatural magic #ALICENOTLEY all this mystery the search for the first woman in alma @almaorthedeadwomen makes me think of the stories i know how important storytelling is 2 my people i'm a daughter of samoa even though i've never been 2 the island i'm samoan i'm afakasi my grandpa helped build the tusitali museum which is both a point of pride & a strange tie it's the museum dedicated 2 robert louis stevenson who is loved by samoa probably because he was a travel writer & wrote fantastic tales about island people & culture & i am like who doesn't like fantastic tales island people & adventure right idk but i feel a little torn those tales are about palagi people coming 2 the islands & taking whatever they want with no consideration for the land but i also wanted 2 be a pirate isn't that romantic & i think about the way the female body has been colonized how history has colonized the body what poems come out of this colonization with what materials is my sound even my own

#ALICENOTLEY what does a witch sound like anne says *according 2 how a person sounds we judge them sane or insane, male or female, good, evil, trustworthy, depressive, marriageable, moribund, likely or unlikely 2 make war on us* @119glassironygod so much of literature is about control the gendering of voice i want 2 know will all the witches speak i say 2 myself in a mirror so i can decide how much better than an animal o that's funny *voice comes directly from the body* @147comingafter & i've trapped it in this room & they want 2 cut our heads off or judge our sound that's just rich i'm trying 2 be sarcastic but my voice isn't right for sarcasm yes that's right alice your reading of gertrude here is important especially when you say what *irritates people about her voice is its insistence on its choice of mannerisms, which seem like idiosyncrasies in the face of more standard expression — how men have said one must say* @153

#ALICENOTLEY let us insist

#ALICENOTLEY i'm bad i'm sorry i've told half a lie i chose heaven because who would choose a representation of a thing when you could have the thing but i'm not sure i believe in heaven isn't that how poems work #ALICENOTLEY you've taught me coming upon a poem is already half a question of belief i've agreed 2 read the poem already i must believe the spell of the poem the enchantment my mom says i should listen 2 the spirits every time she has a dream every time her father comes 2 her in her dreams she warns me i believe dreams are not 2 be messed with i don't believe in god but dreams are real

#ALICENOTLEY every time i dream an unnatural dream i think this is it i've done it now some1 from the death society comes for me

#ALICENOTLEY what is a witch a sound even in opposition to men

#ALICENOTLEY i'll tell you a secret i sometimes pray before i wear my hair down i remember my mom telling me about one of the island ghosts the one that cuts the hair off girls who are snotty who look down at others who walk with their noses up & i promised her i will always walk with my nose down with toilet paper in my pocket i promise i'll never forget what it was like 2 be glad there was bread glad there was saimin glad for whatever free snacks there were at school #ALICENOTLEY i'll tell you another secret because of *the prophet* because you say *all of us know each other* @106 all those books i read were for pizza i never thought of it as free it felt like i was earning something by reading all those books & earning *earning* my stickers eventually adding up 2 food #ALICENOTLEY this is hard it was then too sometimes it still is do you know what i mean the pizza was either four or five slices romantic me thinks it was five which would have been perfect because there were five of us but when i look back on those pictures of my mom from when we were younger when she was younger i know better i know she didn't eat so we could eat when we could & i know i know & there's some kind of angry shame here in my heart i know that sounds stupid perhaps dramatic but feelings are aren't they always feeling so much bigger than they are but my mom my poor mom i didn't realize then that she was starving herself so we could eat & when i think about it

i wish #ALICENOTLEY i wish we all could know each other i wish i believed we could

#ALICENOTLEY i'll tell you another secret when i think about it i feel *bad* like i'm bad like i'm the villain because i never realized isn't that part of it that i should have opened my eyes & i didn't & there was probably so much suffering because of it & i can't go back & fix it i can't go back & i can't fix it & i think it hurt her too when we bought home free pizza there was shame there too something so soul deep it's not even shame really it's just an emptiness you know that feeling when you can't afford something like food so what do you do what do you do

#ALICENOTLEY you have to go on i guess but what do you do

#ALICENOTLEY do witches hold secrets will you hold mine marie says *i don't value brains, poem of the master taxonomy: his same old glow. but it's in the trash. i don't value the trash. i use it. i value myself, keeping on* & i think yes how true & how difficult 2 keep on when institutions authorities in place 2 protect become the threat have always been nurturing whiteness & white supremacy & i know you're thinking reader o no o no she's going 2 say the word patriarchy again & last night #ALICENOTLEY i heard a man say women don't have a place in the history of violence & i well i thought i had better get out of here that's a part of patriarchy & i hear anne here saying *putting a door on the female mouth has been a project of patriarchal culture from antiquity 2 the present* @121glassironyandgod yes you're right *patriarchy* that tyrant whose body we're trying 2 live in i'm of course talking also about the policing of black bodies the news media everyday is filled with the deaths of black people & i think i don't value brains either nor poem of the master taxonomy what's it all for let's throw that poem away write a new poem then at the end of the poem *i judge them guilty, 2 elect themselves again. the woman is gluing the senescent oppressor's creepy love—his paste jewel—2 a tin-can pull ring* @117cultureof1 & it did happen again the election of themselves again & isn't that again basically appropriation except now it can all also happen digitally too & i think god please let's not do that let's use each our voice 2 say black lives matter & i want 2 say also take your creepy love somewhere else somewhere you say @158comingafter poets have 2 be *engaged in a struggle with the truth, or truth as the present reality of this world: how 2 say this world* how indeed 2 say this world when we are erasing it

#ALICENOTLEY a witch is a poet who is struggling how 2 say this world

#ALICENOTLEY where is a witch between *apocalypse & carnival* that's intense like seriously there's some weight there i'm not sure i understand *females who can wreck the infinite* @kristeva as anything other than a title (yet i want 2 be part of whatever it is sounding cool) & i feel witches speak 2 that title i'm thinking about mothers & women who are *split in* 2 you know crone mother maiden too of my own split though i don't feel it except those times its been pointed out once on a bus by a surely nice child *she looks like my doll* once at checkout *what tribe are you from* the too often *where are you from* (me: kc, mo) no *really* where do you come from i'm thinking about the woman i knew as grandmother that sounds formal or something doesn't it i didn't like her she was from my father's side & she would never outright condemn *him* & i wanted him condemned so i was mean unnecessarily hateful even maybe that's dramatic i was afraid being kind 2 her meant somehow 'i'm ok that man your son left us' & also 'i'm okay you've treated my mom poorly' haha the greeks were right it all does go back 2 the father but this isn't that story love for me then was very linearselfish maybe i'm not sure how 2 describe it & maybe i'm imagining this because memory is an experience i thought you had 2 earn love then is that stupid i'm embarrassed 2 tell you this #ALICENOTLEY in your benevolence is that another witchy trait benevolence this from my notes *the frantic doing of everything experience is thought of* @deardarkcontinent that frantic doing of everything captures how i felt then witchy a craft of time how maybe i feel now still the truth is i didn't care that he left it was everything after sometimes i think in our own despair obsessions failings ambitions we forget the ways we affect those around us we forget that no action event moment choice happens in a vacuum

#ALICENOTLEY i remember going 2 a sam's club or hyvee for the first time with my uncle we all went we were so mean when i think about it now we wouldn't take any of the free samples but he ate them i remember him asking what was wrong with us weren't we hungry & yes we were but but i just couldn't i couldn't take it because i knew i'd be taking the sample *because* i was hungry not because i was curious as 2 how whatever-tasted-like i was hungry so i couldn't take the sample isn't that stupid i can hear it now fuck i would hate my 6 year old self what a prude how stupid that sounds eating a privilege any food a treat then & #ALICENOTLEY here's another secret i'm apparently filled with secrets today when he was dying when uncle was dying #ALICENOTLEY all i could think about were those damn samples i refused poor & too proud too proud 2 eat free samples god god what a spoilt child i'm suddenly sorry for everything at the moment when he was dying i wanted more than anything 2 go back 2 that moment at the sam's club or hyvee & eat those samples his hand was so strangely cold not clammy like sweat wet-cold like he'd just been thrown-up from water he'd been drenched but wasn't wet really anymore just chill it was the worst really seeing him there alive-but-gone alive-but-probably-never-coming-back i didn't cry then but i'm crying now i hope all the things people say about heaven really are true i hope there was light i hope he felt loved i hope he knew we loved him i hope heaven is warm i hope it's so warm

#ALICENOTLEY is a witch lucky i think hecate was lucky i'm not sure she's my god but i want 2 shout right now *awesome lady of the annuna gods! crowned with great horns, you fill the heavens and earth with light!* originally one of the seven hymns 2 inanna a witch too @dianewolkstein i like 2 think a daughter of the moon woundn't mind if i invoked her name in deference 2 witches witchcraft magic o that's kind of liberating 2 shout somehow it's strange it feels as if i'm calling down something is the work of a witch 2 invoke #ALICENOTLEY 2 call down something but oh nothing good is ever called down it's all floodflood plagueplague locustfrog floodplaguefrog

#ALICENOTLEY yesterday on twitter i ended all my thoughts with your name & it began 2 feel like an invocation & i thought about what it would be like 2 invoke your name #ALICENOTLEY i invoked so many times i became convinced you heard me saying your name well not me specifically just that you knew your name was being called 2 then i got a chill & i was sure of it sure you #ALICENOTLEY are hearing everything

#ALICENOTLEY can a witch hear *everything* my mom says when you sneeze someone is talking about you & when i wake up sometimes #ALICENOTLEY this is a tiny secret sometimes i whisper i love you mom & i think i should say this everyday & i hope she sneezes everyday but never catches a cold

#ALICENOTLEY jane says *magic was no hole & corner practice but an affair of public ritual performed with full social sanction…magic was of the state, not of the individual* & then she asks *what exactly is this public social magic?* @77 @janeellenharrison & i wonder what you would say because the epic is a public poem isn't it about public things war grief loss the human cost the human hurt an uttered desire words spoken out loud again an invocation a prayer i am curious too if magic is a public concern could it be abused or could it do the most healing like rain or baked bread honestly i don't like being rained on #ALICENOTLEY witches are weird & poetry is weird it's private & also i-want-2-share-this with you isn't this a convo poets have all the time it's kind of boring kind of important i don't know it does occupy a public space here i'm thinking about claudia rankine's *words encoding the bodies they cover. and despite everything the body remains* @69citizen & also anne waldman's *process of restoring poetry 2 health* @85comingafter they have this public voice alice you say poetry *uses personal feeling & knowledge 2 achieve a public voice that's thoughtful enough, playful enough & subtle enough, 2 appeal 2 a reader or audience member as an individual intelligence without separating her/him from others, from communal issues* @106comingafter #ALICENOTLEY & marie has this achieved this public voice too as the word is telling her that *the man set fire 2 my house, because he wanted 2* @53cultureof1 i think the absence poetry responds 2 & uses as its material the materiality of the lines that fractured sense of self which isn't reflected anywhere so powerfully than in a poem maybe poems making room 2 talk about intersecting oppressions it gives you permission 2 talk about how words stick 2 the real @spicer what's left out in the making of that real who is where are the silences what are they saying

#ALICENOTLEY a witch uses magic if magic is a thing 2 use how do we always put it in service of compassion you say poetry is compassion is poetry a kind of magic #ALICENOTLEY is magic are witches compassionate

#ALICENOTLEY what is a mystery & does it have anything 2 do with the divine & does that really have anything 2 do with the supernatural is this the same question what is a witch #ALICENOTLEY i felt compelled 2 tell you a whole bunch of things but i've only accomplished questions

#ALICENOTLEY is a witch a healer

#ALICENOTLEY is a witch a healer can power be constructive & destructive

#ALICENOTLEY is the power of a witch destructive

#ALICENOTLEY a witch is magic magic is some emotion an emotion is some desire some longing an invisible gravitation towards what *constructive or destructive* @85 @janeellenharrison *not passive but active* magic is active #ALICENOTLEY makes it sound like a responsibility is it i immediately recoil if so i don't think i'm responsible enough for that kind of responsibility if i'm disobedient 2 everything though then my allegiance is 2 the poem i question my allegiances am i disobedient enough

#ALICENOTLEY i'm not breaking any lines i wonder if there's drama here if it's all just pitch flat

#ALICENOTLEY a silence has settled over the room & i am trying 2 listen 2 see if there's something in the silence i recognize i wonder if i'm being watched i remember claudia said the other day she believed in angels i wasn't sure what 2 say my mom believes in angels too my sister does too but she also believes in ufos which i admittedly said sarcastically because i don't really trust 'progress in the name of science' it's unfair of me really i can believe in dreams in spirits yet i'm not sure about angels my mom says the spirit of my grandfather was with me during that tornado he told her i'd be okay i was i can't believe in angels because i can't believe in god wouldn't those go hand in hand here i turn 2 mary with *why all our literary pursuits are useless* (the answer is nature) *eighty-five percent of all existing species are beetles & various forms of insects. english is spoken by only 5 percent of the world's population* @247

#ALICENOTLEY i want 2 be a witch i want magic

#ALICENOTLEY i see it's always about emotion power 2 speak from those scars like marie like alette who found power in her ritual death—*"talons tore me," "tore my flesh," "as i was dragged" "n2 the darkness" "the pain was on fire in" "spreading pools," "quick-opening flowers," "fiery blossoms" "with torn" "pecked centers" "till all i was was fire" "fire &" "screaming" "but soon" "there was no pain" "there was numbness" "& an eating" "an eating of" "my body"* @209—power who found her name & her body & asks *also what is it like at the beginning of the world* it gives me hope when you say a poem may not change the world right away but it'll *be* & so in its presence it informs transforms activates the space

#ALICENOTLEY is a witch ever nervous

#ALICENOTLEY i'm nervous all the time i'm nervous you're reading this even if you don't ever know my name i know once once you said it out loud

173

#ALICENOTLEY every time i hear the word cow i think about gertrude & nancy krusoe though they don't agree on what a cow actually is gertrude uses cow 2 say orgasm it was her secret word with other alice i'm a little in love with it as a monosyllable cow cow i can imagine alice let's cow cow cow cow cow for nancy was just what you might expect the animal i've written this in my notebook *like her, i became a cow & i became a mother. i became the barn & the hill, the lake & the water cows drink from the lake, the salt & the saliva in their mouths. i became, for a while, entirely these things—nothing more. & this is not enough* @frommynotebook & i think about how for these women who were ghouls too it's never enough is it it'll never be enough & i know what you mean when you say #ALICENOTLEY *there is no audience because there is no audience* @84 & my god #ALICENOTLEY i am in tears i can't help it i don't know how 2 fix it how 2 unwound

#ALICENOTLEY let us pray together both dead & alive & live is a witch being after all we're in the time of the poem aren't we claudia aren't we always isn't that witch's time the poet's time medea's time dido's time my time your time & your time #ALICENOTLEY your time is witch's time mystic time when i open the book i'm in that time in the interior of the book time is interior when you ask *are you in it yet, here, this magic/ nothing's in balance* @69 & i shout yes yes! i'm here medea #ALICENOTLEY i'm here

#ALICENOTLEY is being a ghoul like being a vampire can you make me a ghoul
or if i want it enough am i already a ghoul am i already a ghoul there's a mystery
here is a witch a ghoul i want 2 be a nighthag a demigorgon

#ALICENOTLEY i'm thinking about annie dillard do you like annie dillard i am the most curious i'm thinking about *words* about *mystery* again about *magic* #ALICENOTLEY you are magic & is death magic some transference of energy & nature is magic isn't it all those seasons all that magical blooming unthawing splashing *our life* says annie *is a faint tracing on the surface of mystery, like the idle, curved tunnels of leaf miners on the face of a leaf. we must somehow take a wider view, look at the whole landscape, really see it, & describe what's going on here. then we can at least wail the right question n2 the swaddling band of darkness, or, if it comes 2 that, choir the proper praise @245* #ALICENOTLEY is annie a witch there's that darkness again the light flickers or someone walks by i don't know the right question but i am somehow getting along you are right annie you are right #ALICENOTLEY as i step back

#ALICENOTLEY it is dark let us stay here dark nestled nestled by the dark let us grow here in this dark i grow in this dark i had a dream for nine days the dark rains down everything becomes dark is coated in the dark & i think how good it is that i've learned 2 see in the dark how good it is that i've made a home here in the dark out of nothing how good it is that i've handed over authority that i trust the poem

Thanks to the editors and journals that published a version of these poems—
Dream Pop Press, Gigantic Sequins, Split Lip Magazine, Denver Quarterly

Featuring—Alice Notley, Audre Lorde, Adrienne Rich, Helene Cixous, Julia
Kristeva, Judith Butler, Jane Ellen Harrison, Wikipedia, Sylvia Plath, Virginia
Woolf, Claudia Rankine, Patricia Hill Collins, Anne Carson, HD, Plato, Megan
Thee Stallion, Ovid, Louis-Ferdinand Celine, Emily Dickinson, Diane Wolkstein,
Mary Ruefle, Gertrude Stein, Anne Waldman, Annie Dillard

Leia Penina Wilson is proudly Samoan. When she's not reading trashy
paranormal romance novels or puzzling, she plays *Magic the Gathering* (edh).
Her favorite commander is Olivia Voldaren. Other favorites include Sailor Moon,
Donatello, cinnamon tea, *Gargoyles*, cake, ice cream, *Diablo, Dragon Age*,
mangoes, rice pudding, coconut, and watermelon.

this red metropolis what remains
Leia Penina Wilson

Cover image: *Anguish* (1878) by August Friedrich Schenck

Cover and interior set in Wittenberger Fraktur MT Std and Electra LT Std

Cover and interior design by Gillian Olivia Blythe Hamel

Printed in the United States
by Bookmobile, Minneapolis, Minnesota
On Rolland Enviro Book 55# 446 ppi Natural 100% PCW
Acid Free Archival Quality Recycled Paper

Publication of this book was made possible in part by gifts from
Katherine & John Gravendyk in honor of Hillary Gravendyk,
Francesca Bell, Mary Mackey, and The New Place Fund

Omnidawn Publishing
Oakland, California
Staff and Volunteers, Fall 2020

Rusty Morrison & Ken Keegan, senior editors & co-publishers
Kayla Ellenbecker, production editor & poetry editor
Gillian Olivia Blythe Hamel, senior editor & book designer
Trisha Peck, senior editor & book designer
Rob Hendricks, *Omniverse* editor, marketing editor & post-pub editor
Cassandra Smith, poetry editor & book designer
Sharon Zetter, poetry editor & book designer
Liza Flum, poetry editor
Matthew Bowie, poetry editor
Jason Bayani, poetry editor
Juliana Paslay, fiction editor
Gail Aronson, fiction editor
Izabella Santana, fiction editor & marketing assistant
Laura Joakimson, marketing assistant specializing in Instagram & Facebook
Ashley Pattison-Scott, executive assistant & *Omniverse* writer
Ariana Nevarez, marketing assistant & *Omniverse* writer
SD Sumner, copyeditor